PRAISE FOR THE SMART THINKING BOOK

"Short, direct and powerful."
Seth Godin, Author

"World class trainer."
Diana Rhodes, Head of Strategy & Planning,
Royal Mail MarketReach

**"When you want to take your mind for a sprint,
pack *The Smart Thinking Book* as your protein bar."**
Richard Hytner, Deputy Chairman, Saatchi & Saatchi Worldwide, and author of *Consiglieri*

**"A fast, no bullshit shot in the arm for all of us who forget
how simple business can be. Punchy + Bouncy = Refreshing!"**
Chris Baréz-Brown, Founder of Upping Your Elvis, and author of *Shine* and *Free!*

**"So many business books comprise a few good ideas and
a lot of padding. Kevin's book is full of a lot of good ideas
and NO padding. Which would you prefer?"**
Euan Semple, ex-BBC, and author of *Organizations Don't Tweet, People Do*

**"I like my fiction meandering and time consuming.
I like my non-fiction informative and straight to the point.
Kevin's book meets the second criteria admirably –
simple valuable messages, efficiently conveyed."**
George Cooper, author of *Money, Blood and Revolution*

**"Another gem from the King of Common Sense.
Kevin has beautifully captured the most common challenges
that we all encounter in our business lives, and distilled them
down to their most fundamental parts, and offered a variety
of possible solutions. Invaluable and inspirational."**
Chris Carmichael, Global Head of Media, HSBC

TO:

ROSANNA, SHAUNAGH

AND SARAH

Thanks for comment on the early draft:
Chris Barez-Brown, Chris Carmichael, Katy Clarkson,
George Cooper, Rosie Duncan, Seth Godin, Richard Hytner,
Euan Semple, Rory Sutherland, Dawn Sillett and Dave Trott.

Thanks to my wife Sarah
for helping me plan the book on the wall.

Thanks to Jim Collins and Seth Godin
for their words of encouragement.

THE
SMART
THINKING
BOOK

OVER 70 BURSTS
OF BUSINESS BRILLIANCE

KEVIN DUNCAN

MADRID | MEXICO CITY | LONDON
NEW YORK | BUENOS AIRES
BOGOTA | SHANGHAI | NEW DELHI

Published by
LID Publishing Limited
The Record Hall, Studio 304,
16-16a Baldwins Gardens,
London EC1N 7RJ, UK

info@lidpublishing.com
www.lidpublishing.com

A member of:

businesspublishersroundtable.com

© Kevin Duncan, 2021
© LID Publishing Limited, 2021
First edition published in 2015

Printed in Latvia by Jelgavas Tipogrāfija

ISBN: 978-1-912555-84-0
ISBN: 978-1-911671-25-1 (ebook)

Cover design: Matthew Renaudin

CONTENTS

PART SIX: THINKING

INTRODUCTION

It's always fun to reissue a book, as we have done already with the fifth-anniversary editions of *The Diagrams Book* and *The Ideas Book*.

And it is instructive to read again something that you wrote a while ago.

Looking at *The Smart Thinking Book*, I believe the provocations are as relevant as ever.

With everyone so frantically busy, most people are keen to pick up intelligent ideas fast.

I have added new material in every section, so there are now over 70 bursts of business intelligence.

You can read the whole thing in a little over an hour, or each thought in one minute.

Each provocation is ideal for sticking on the wall, scrutinizing fast with some colleagues (or on your own), and working out how to galvanize your business or project with a new angle.

Good luck applying them to your work, and do let me know how you get on with these ideas.

Kevin Duncan, Westminster 2021

A WORD ON GROWTH

Most companies are obsessed by growth, but blindly pursuing it isn't the smartest idea in every context.

Plans and models are frequently wrong, and hitting the target often involves missing the point.

Direction, destination and movement all require careful thought, otherwise there may well be a lot going on but little of the right sort of progress being made.

Flexibility and clarity are vital to achieving the right type of growth, and that includes being absolutely clear about what you are *not* going to do.

Remove all distractions, and then tenaciously stick to the few things that will really make a difference.

As Kurt Vonnegut once said, "A step backward, after making a wrong turn, is a step in the right direction."

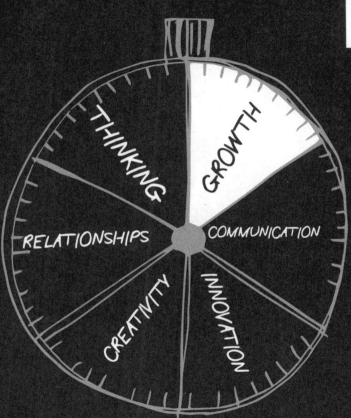

PART ONE

ALL PLANS
ARE
FICTION

A plan is just a plan. Just because it is written down, it doesn't mean that's what is going to happen.

"No battle plan survives contact with the enemy," according to Colin Powell, the former US Secretary of State.

In other words, planning is theoretical.

And there's a lot of difference between theory and practice.

Mike Tyson had a more blunt way of putting it.

"Everybody has a plan until they get punched in the face."

Everything changes all the time. So the bulk of assumptions made at the planning stage may well be wrong.

In fact, they usually are.

"A good plan violently executed now is better than a perfect plan executed next week," said the famous military commander George S. Patton.

So the best approach is to draw up a reasonable plan, fast, and then get on with it.

ALL
MODELS
ARE
WRONG

According to statistician George Box:
"All models are wrong, but some are useful."

A model is just a representation.

Models are usually simplified, often to the point
of being simplistic.

As mathematician Alfred North Whitehead said:
"Seek simplicity and distrust it."

Many business people make the mistake of
assuming that the model they have drawn up is
how reality will turn out.

It isn't.

It's just a guide. A suggestion. A shape.

So next time you are presented with a model,
challenge it.

And next time you are designing one,
don't necessarily believe it.

A target is just a target.

It's something to aim at, but you might not hit it.

A percentage is just a percentage.
A percentage of what?

1% of a lot might be a lot. 99% of not very
much might be... not very much.

So arbitrarily adding 10% to last year's target
may well be pointless.

There is absolute performance, and there is
relative performance.

Absolute performance is what *you* want to achieve.

Relative performance compares yours with
the competition.

Do you really care what *they* do?

Or would you rather concentrate on your own
intentions and aspirations?

By all means set targets, but do it on your own terms.

Direction is a line or a course.

It goes a certain way.

It's not the same as the destination.

Barely any journey, whether physical or temporal, follows a single straight line.

Most involve a number of directions, plural.

So your direction today may well be different from your direction tomorrow, even though the destination remains the same.

Smart business people understand that many directions are needed to reach the ultimate destination.

Don't confuse the two.

DON'T CONFUSE MOVEMENT WITH PROGRESS

Just because a lot is going on it doesn't mean that you are actually getting anywhere.

Some people, and businesses generally, love having lots of people rushing around.

It makes them feel productive.

Regardless of what they are doing, all the frenetic activity suggests that much helpful work is being done.

People even say sometimes that they like the buzz.

But it's a bit like a goalkeeper diving to save a penalty.

He might be just as effective staying exactly where he is.

So movement doesn't necessarily mean progress.

Don't confuse the two.

You need to be doing the *right* things.

WHEN
THE FACTS
CHANGE,
CHANGE YOUR
MIND

It is good to have a clear point of view.

If you aspire to being an effective manager, this is precisely what's needed.

It rallies staff around a cause, and explains what you are trying to do.

But things rarely go exactly as planned.

New information emerges all the time.

So the smart leader needs to realize when to change.

It's painful to watch someone who is wedded to an approach and won't adjust.

Circumstances have changed, but they won't.

They stubbornly stick to the original plan.

As the economist John Maynard Keynes observed:

"When the facts change, I change my mind. What do you do?"

Panicking isn't ideal, but if you are going to do it, then do so early in the process.

The traditional student essay crisis approach does not work well in business.

Doing too little for too long and then bursting into random or poorly directed activity is not effective.

Too many briefs and tasks sit in in-trays until they become fiendishly difficult to answer or solve.

So next time you have a complex task, be sure to panic early.

Gather all the personnel that matter within the first 24 hours, generate an approach, and set it in motion.

You can always adjust later.

And for those who say they work better under pressure: you don't.

Most business people and companies have far too much to do.

Or at least it appears that way. But much of what they are doing could be described as 'administrivia'.

The more tasks we are given, the more important it becomes to work out what is truly worth doing, and what is not.

Most status reports and activity sheets have far too much on them.

This may make individuals and companies feel that they are being diligent.

But in truth it is more likely to be blurring their view of what really matters.

Concentrate on action, not activity.

Cull as many projects and tasks as possible.

Often, one single action can utterly transform a project or task.

Take the time to work out what that specific single action is, and just do that.

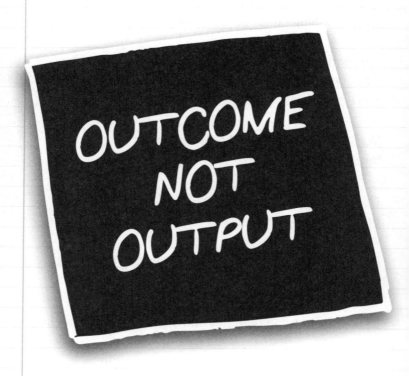

The amount of things that a company or an individual does is irrelevant.

No one ever said: "What a great project that was — it took over 500 meetings to get it done."

It's the outcome that matters, not the output.

So the question is not: "How much can we get done?"

The question is: "What is the easiest way to achieve our desired outcome?"

At the beginning of every project or task, put the emphasis on this question.

If you spend proper time doing that, then the rest will follow naturally.

And the outcome will arrive faster.

An Anti List is a list of things that you are *not* going to do.

This is a crucial aid in establishing what you *are* going to do.

Such a list establishes:

What you will *never* do.

What you don't *want* to do.

What you won't be doing in the near future.

All three perspectives are important in determining where growth will come from.

The first sets up principles to which the company can adhere.

The second flushes out desire and motivation.

The third determines priority.

Match the Anti List to the conventional task list and you have a powerful formula to provide your business with a clear centre of gravity for the coming year.

"If I stop to kick every barking dog, I'm not going to get where I'm going."

That's the view of Jackie Joyner-Kersee, one of the most successful Olympic athletes ever.

In other words, if you are striving for excellence, then you want as few distractions as possible – preferably none.

So that means being absolutely clear about how you intend to achieve growth and what you will sacrifice in order to get those things done.

There will always be events and people blocking or derailing your work, but they need to be vigorously resisted so that you can retain focus on what's important.

As George Bernard Shaw said: "People who say it cannot be done should not interrupt those who are doing it."

Five frogs are sitting on a log. One decides to jump off. How many frogs are now on the log?

Most people answer four, but the right answer is five. Just because someone decides to do something doesn't mean that they have done it.

As the brilliant American aviator Amelia Earhart said: "The most difficult thing is the decision to act; the rest is merely tenacity."

So the first thing to do is decide, and then get on with it. But speed doesn't always pay. According to the actor and choreographer André De Shields: "Slow is the fastest way to get where you want to go."

Sticking to the task doggedly is the most important component of forward motion and progress.

A WORD ON COMMUNICATION

There is nothing that can't be misunderstood, so it is essential to make sure that everybody really does understand what you intend to communicate.

Make sure that you have a genuine point. State it clearly and then pay deep attention to people's reactions to it.

Cut out the waffle and bullshit to get to the true essence of what needs to be expressed.

Package messages in easily digestible quantities and make them sharp, not fluffy.

Surround yourself with smart people who will tell you everything you might want to consider, and then adjust your approach based on the collective intelligence generated by combined thinking.

As George Bernard Shaw said, "The single biggest problem in communication is the illusion that it has taken place."

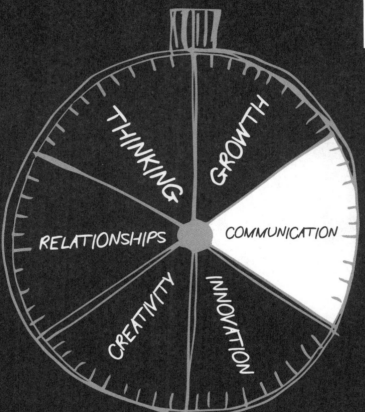

PART TWO

There is no point in talking unless you have a point.

Too many people are, literally, pointless.

But it doesn't stop them talking.

Despite having no point, no point of view, and no line of argument, they start talking.

According to Princeton professor Harry G. Frankfurt: "Bullshit is stimulated whenever a person's obligations or opportunities to speak about some topic exceed their knowledge of the facts that are relevant to the topic."

In other words, they don't know what they are talking about.

Contrary to popular business belief, it's perfectly fine to say: "I don't know."

So, next time you are inclined to speak on a topic, make sure you have a genuine point.

ROI:
RESPECT = OPINION
+ INQUIRY

When A.G. Lafley returned as Chief Executive of Procter & Gamble for the second time, he was appalled to find that most of the meetings he attended contained over 20 people.

He set about changing them in three ways.

No presentations were allowed (only a discussion of strategic issues agreed in advance), a maximum of five people in the room, and no more than three pages of new material in response to queries.

He also introduced a new discussion style called assertive inquiry, which blends advocacy (what I think) with inquiry (listen properly).

This is best summarized in the sentence:

"I have a view worth hearing, but I may be missing something."

This approach encourages well-informed confidence, but stops short of overconfidence.

And it encourages teamwork by requiring people to listen to the views of their colleagues.

So the right attitude is to blend opinion with inquiry.

Generating things to do makes companies
feel productive, but many tasks may not
be worth doing.

Projects often take on a life of their own.

A lot of people rush around but no one has stopped
to ask one of the most important questions of all:
Do we really need to do this?

This question is not cynical, nor is it an
attempt to avoid work.

It is a vital line of inquiry to find out if what is being
done has a clear purpose.

The upshot of not pausing to ask is that teams,
and even whole companies, can slip into a groove
of 'doing' rather than thinking.

And that doing eventually becomes "the way we
do things round here."

Which could be a very dangerous thing.

As the comedy character Alan B'Stard famously
observed: "Bollocks today - policy tomorrow."

Companies are full of people who bullshit,
but they are not necessarily liars.

They are phony rather than false.

They are faking things, but that doesn't necessarily
mean they get things wrong.

The bullshitter has much more freedom than
someone who tells the truth or lies, because they
do not require an anchor point on one side
or the other.

This does not mean rejecting the authority
of truth, as the liar does, or even opposing it.

It means paying no attention to it at all.

In the bullshit vortex, entire teams and companies
can spend thousands of hours just picking out
material, or making it up, to suit their purpose.

In amongst all this, they are not necessarily
getting anywhere.

If this is happening in your company,
it's time to ban the bull.

Ask anyone whether there are any wafflers
in their company and many will say yes.

Some confess to doing it themselves.

Most do it because they have an unformulated
idea taking shape in their head that they cannot
articulate in the spoken word.

Others do it when asked a question, and simply
start talking regardless of whether they have
anything helpful to say.

In some companies, this process repeats itself
all day and contributes to an unproductive
working environment.

This needs to stop.

For every waffler, there is a wafflee – someone
who has to listen to this drivel.

Wafflers need to rein it in. Instead of springing
a spontaneous word dump on someone, ask them:

"I have a roughly formulated idea I'd like to discuss
with you for five minutes. When is convenient for you?"

Telling the truth makes your life easier.

For a start, you don't ever have to remember
what you said, because you never lied.

Companies do too much lying.

Liars are unpleasant to be around.

And yet delivering news straight can
be fraught too.

As Noel Coward said:

"It's discouraging to think how many people
are shocked by honesty and how few by deceit."

When it comes to keeping people informed, you are
better off replacing a trickle of doubt with
a flood of naked truth.

Because, as historian C. Northcote Parkinson observed:

"The void created by the failure to communicate is
soon filled with poison, drivel and misrepresentation."

The animation company Pixar, creators of *Finding Nemo* and *Toy Story*, has a proven formula for successful storytelling.

What has become known as the Pixar Pitch involves six sequential sentences:

Once upon a time, A.

Every day, B.

One day, C.

Because of that, D.

Because of that, E.

Until finally, F.

All successful communication blends this kind of appeal with flexibility.

Getting the order right is critical for clear explanation.

And the power of the sequence ensures that your audience comes along with you.

"It's not what you say, it's what people hear."

So said American political pollster Frank Luntz.

And he's right.

This works in two directions.

First, almost everything anyone says can be completely misunderstood.

When you are communicating something, bear this in mind, especially if you are addressing a large audience.

Secondly though, do not patronize your audience by assuming they won't get it. They probably will.

If your message involves some complex technical detail, don't fudge or gloss over it.

Instead find an engaging way to explain it.

It's your job to ensure clear comprehension.

The author and journalist Rebecca West famously asserted: "There is no such thing as conversation. It is an illusion. There are intersecting monologues, that is all."

Let's assume we are not all as cynical as her.

Conversation is not a monologue. It's two-way.

So it's a deal of sorts. You make yourself understood.

Then you pay attention carefully to what the other person is saying.

You assimilate that response, and then you adjust your next remarks accordingly.

Many people become flustered by this. They just keep on transmitting.

But remember, the other person is waiting for your response.

So instead of diving in with any old rubbish just to fill the silence, try leaving a big pause.

They have to wait because they asked a question. And you get time to think and say something thoughtful.

In the Jazz Café music venue in London, there are four letters painted onto a pillar by the stage.

STFU.

That means Shut The F*#k Up.

So the artistes can be heard properly.

You might think that's just jazz musicians for you.

But even the philosopher Simone Weil said:

"Attention is the rarest and purest form of generosity."

So if you really want to help out a colleague, give them your time and proper attention.

Two things always bedevil businesses: first, most discussions, presentations and documents are too long; and second, in many instances, the purpose of a project or task is so diffuse that people don't know what they are doing.

So when it comes to communication, there are two vital components: a sharp, clear brief at the beginning, and a short, pithy recommendation.

Everything has the capacity to be misunderstood. As the old saying goes: "I know that you believe you understand what you think I said, but I am not sure you realize that what you heard is not what I meant."

In your work, if it is within your power, resist the following at all costs: having no clear brief or objective; long, rambling conversations that lead nowhere; and overly long presentations that leave everyone bewildered.

For best communication, marry evidence with a little emotion and evocative expression. Sharpness is acuity. Keep it pithy and punchy, and avoid the empty vacuum of vacuity.

A discussion should be an exchange of views, not two intersecting monologues.

Too few people listen, and without listening, it is impossible to build consensus and agree direction.

Intelligence and consideration for others are vital here.

Communication cannot be effective if people with entrenched views simply dig their heels in.

As Brian Clough, the famous football manager, said: "Don't argue with idiots. They'll bring you down to their level and then beat you with experience."

Of course, some people are not only stubborn but also downright aggressive in their views.

Author Hans Rosling was given this piece of advice by a governor in Tanzania: "When someone threatens you with a machete, never turn your back. Stand still. Look him straight in the eye. And ask him what the problem is."

This is sound counsel. Defuse communication blockages by pausing to ask what the problem is.

Listen carefully to the response and use it to build a basis of understanding and a potential way forward.

A WORD ON INNOVATION

Being relentlessly curious and wanting to solve things that don't work well are at the root of innovation.

Old thinking won't do, so the past should be ignored to make progress. We are looking for progress, not perfection.

Plan A almost never works, so it is important to be open-minded about many alternatives.

Act yourself into a new way of thinking by prototyping products or bodystorming services.

And sometimes a simple 'adjacent possible' – the simplest next step – is sufficient to make progress.

Pure originality is less important than sensible enhancement, and many products are over-specified, so learn to work out when enough is enough.

As author Graham Greene once said, "Sometimes I wonder how all those who do not write, compose or paint can manage to escape the madness, the melancholia, the panic and fear which is inherent to the human condition."

PART THREE

A lot of people think that those who come up with inspired ideas are either supremely talented or just plain lucky.

Neither is necessarily true, and it is possible to increase your chances of being innovative.

It all starts with being relentlessly curious.

You have to be intrinsically interested in a wide range of things.

Become a mental magpie, regularly picking up many stimuli.

When you have a tricky task or problem, you are effectively briefing your depth mind.

In due course, in what is sometimes called "The Unconcealing", your brain will attach an interesting observation to the task in hand.

That's not luck, nor plain serendipity.

It's a direct result of applying your curiosity to an issue.

That's how innovations emerge.

In the comedy programme of the same name, Father Ted tries in vain to explain to his hapless assistant the apparent size difference between objects (in this case a cow) that are close and far away.

"The Adjacent Possible" was a phrase coined by scientist Stuart Kauffman.

It refers to the nearest next steps that can be made in relation to any challenge.

It is always the best place to start when trying to innovate.

Far too many innovation challenges veer off into strange areas that are either impossible or undesirable to enact.

So begin the process by mapping out the elements closest to the subject.

Then work out the simplest next thing to do to expand outward from the centre.

Finding an opportunity that is close is always easier than one that is far away.

It's hard to move on when you, or a colleague, keep referring back to the past.

What happened before is only of passing interest.

Much more important is what is happening now or in the future.

So when it comes to generating new ideas, you need to forget the past.

As strategist and writer Adam Morgan says: "Break with your immediate past."

Or, put another way, forget everything you know and think again.

This approach is good for sweeping away the cobwebs of old thinking to allow a truly unfettered basis for fresh thinking.

It can also be a very useful rule in any idea generation or brainstorm session.

Nothing is perfect, and yet any meeting or company will almost certainly include some people who claim to be perfectionists.

Some perfectionists are defensive, and say they do it because no one else has standards as high as theirs.

But most perfectionists usually say that they do not like being that way, but can't help it.

Subordinates dread having a perfectionist boss, because nothing is ever good enough for them (apparently).

Their work is usually altered by their boss, so they often give up trying.

Perfectionists put additional pressure on their colleagues by taking far longer to complete work, with faster staff usually picking up the slack.

So, what to do?

Go for progress, not perfection.

Give it your best shot and then make it happen.

Planning is often a mirage.

There's nothing wrong with having a finely crafted Plan A, but the chances of it happening in precisely that fashion are low.

So you need a Plan B.

And quite possibly a Plan C, D, E and so on.

Some people, and companies, become very frustrated when Plan A turns out to be ineffective.

This is usually because they have a high level of emotional investment in it.

But that is a poorly informed approach.

Because if Plan A is shown to be flawed, then there is no point in carrying on with it.

And the good news is that Plan B may well turn out to be *better* than Plan A.

People love sitting around talking about strategy.

It gives them an excuse to drink coffee and eat biscuits on company time.

But strategy is just a grand sounding word for what you have decided to do.

Unless you get on and do it, you're just talking.

Old academic joke: "Yes it works in practice, but does it work in theory?"

So, if your team or company spends too much time talking and not enough time doing, then they could do worse than heed this observation from business writer Richard Pascale.

"People are much more likely to act their way into a new way of thinking than think their way into a new way of acting."

In other words, once the thinking is done, stop talking and get on with it.

Then you'll really know if it works in practice.

Anyone can sit in a room and say
"Wouldn't it be great if...?"

To which the reasonable answer is: "Yes it would.
Can you make it work?"

This is where many a so-called brilliant idea
comes unstuck.

And it hasn't even reached the drawing board.

Making rough prototypes of proposed products cuts
to the chase fast and can avoid months or even
years of talk.

If it's a physical product, construct a rough working
version to show how it will work.

You will soon find out if it has merit.

If it's a service idea, then act it out to see if it works.

This is called 'bodystorming': using physical actions
to bring an idea in a brainstorm to life.

Fast and early prototyping improves any
innovation process.

Speed kills, or so the saying goes.

No it doesn't, at least according to Jeremy Clarkson.

"Speed never killed anyone. Suddenly becoming stationary, that's what gets you."

All projects benefit from momentum.

It's human nature.

We start off very excited with our new toy.

And then we have a motivational dip.

You can even plot the likely energy and enthusiasm curve of a project before it starts.

So don't hang around letting bureaucracy and inertia set in.

Grasp the initial energy of the new idea and run with it as fast as possible.

And you'll know if it's a winner sooner than if you let it lag.

RTFM. It stands for Read The F*@#king Manual.

This priceless acronym was the invention of exasperated engineers when trying to help clueless operators.

Those operators were invariably asking inane questions about how the product in question worked.

But they hadn't had the diligence to read the manual first.

If they had, then they would have had a better chance of knowing what they were doing.

Far too many people, and companies, try to wing it.

They pretty much make it up as they go along.

Occasionally it works, but usually it doesn't.

It's at this point that RTFM is extremely good advice.

Follow the process. Get trained properly.

Learn the details of the item in question.

Then proceed from a position of knowledge rather than ignorance.

Fool's gold looks like gold, but it isn't.

It's usually some other yellow mineral like pyrite or chalcopyrite.

White space is blank, and when it's on a strategist's market map, it makes them think there's a gap to be exploited.

But they might be wrong, particularly when it comes to innovations.

'Fool's gold white space' is an apparent gap in the market, but in truth it's a failure masquerading as a viable opportunity.

Many an innovator has been fooled by it.

So next time you come across what appears to be an unoccupied area, ask yourself two questions.

Why is this space unoccupied?

What do they know that we don't?

According to American comedian Bo Burnham:
"Original doesn't mean good."

And he's right. Something original could just
as easily be bad or indifferent.

So innovation doesn't have to be blindingly
original – it just needs to make a helpful step in
a better direction.

Sometimes this comes from frustration with
something that doesn't work very well: how can
we improve it?

On other occasions, a new or previously unforeseen
need is waiting to be fulfilled.

The problem is that, by definition, innovation
includes something that is new. So there is a strong
chance that we don't know what we are doing.
As TV presenter James Richardson points out:
"Nothing important comes with instructions."

So, we have to work it out through trial and error.

It's all about small steps and that adjacent possible.

Philosopher Epicurus wisely noted that:
"Nothing is enough for the man to whom enough is too little."

There is too much clutter in the world, and a huge proportion of products are over-specified.

So, we need to recognize when enough is enough.

Socrates, who died 50 years before Epicurus was born, decreed on entering a marketplace:
"What a lot of things are here that I don't need."

All we need is what is sufficient. And when it comes to products and services, the less extraneous stuff the better.

It's what the designer Raymond Loewy called "MAYA": Most Advanced Yet Acceptable.

In other words, push the boundaries a bit, but don't overdo it.

A WORD ON CREATIVITY

Creativity thrives in stimulating environments,
so make sure you provide one.

In the fuzzy front end, everything is a mess.
Don't worry about this – it's essential for making
unexpected connections.

Start by generating way more ideas than will ultimately
be needed, then be ruthless in editing them down.

Don't innovate all the time – it's exhausting and
distracting. Beware novelty overload, and remember
that quitting can be winning.

And don't expect inspiration to strike miraculously
– it doesn't. Instead, get to work and good things
will follow.

Then once you alight on something genuinely innovative,
pursue it with total conviction.

Novelist Madeleine L'Engle once said, "Inspiration
usually comes during work, rather than before it."

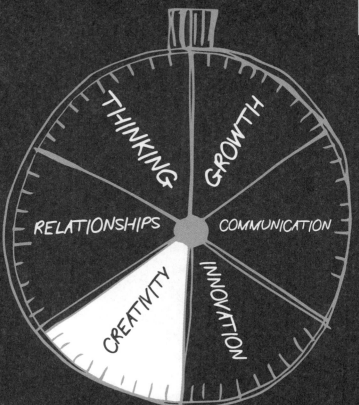

PART FOUR

Creativity needs a decent place to flourish.

And yet many offices are sterile environments.

Air conditioning. Poor light, or no natural light.
Airless basements.

This is no place to be inventive, let alone
hold a brainstorm.

Research shows that people have more ideas when
the ceiling is high and if the walls are painted blue.

It reminds them of unfettered nature —
a world with no boundaries.

As the famous explorer Thor Heyerdahl
once remarked:

"Borders? I have never seen one. But I have
heard they exist in the minds of some people."

So if you crave creativity, create an
environment to help.

And that means a greenhouse where ideas
can grow and be nurtured.

The fuzzy front end is a phrase often used to describe the messy uncertain bit at the beginning of any project.

At this stage it may not be particularly evident how things are going to progress, or how it's all going to come together.

Don't panic. It's normal in any creative endeavour.

In fact, as business author Max McKeown points out:

"The fuzziness never really leaves as long as you are attempting to do something new."

In fact, he argues, there's often a fuzzy middle bit and a fuzzy back end as well.

So relax into it.

The best creative cultures and individuals are comfortable with ambiguity.

As Aristotle noted:

"It is the mark of an educated mind to be able to entertain a thought without accepting it."

All creativity involves some form of shot in the dark.

Discovery consists of seeing what everyone has seen and thinking what nobody has thought.

A leap from A to B, often via a somewhat unexpected C.

Small, incremental development of something that is already well established usually fails to provide sufficient differentiation.

So an element of destruction is needed.

Start by utterly 'destroying' the current version, solution, product, or whatever it is you are grappling with.

Clear the decks and try starting again.

Approach the challenge from two very different directions.

What *do* I know about it?

What *don't* I know about it?

Somewhere in the answers to those two questions lies a new originality.

It is fashionable to regard having lots of ideas as
an indicator of a healthy business.

But it's not necessarily the number of ideas
that matters.

It's how good they are.

And whether they ever get done.

In many cases, concentrating on too many
ideas spreads resources too thinly.

And that can be as detrimental to success
as not having many ideas at all.

So, don't just get rid of the bad ideas.

Kill some good ones as well.

Especially if they are not quite good enough.

This will leave all the available resource free
to concentrate on those that have the potential
to be truly great.

Sometimes quantity is the first step when generating creative ideas.

Out of a large volume of suggestions comes something workable and better.

If that's the case, then the language used in creative conversations can have a deep bearing on whether you and your team are likely to get anywhere.

Roger Martin, one of the great innovation and design thinkers of recent times, expressed this as:

"Managers need to take Ors and turn them into Ands."

In other words, instead of saying, "We could do this or this," the discussion should concentrate on "We could do this *and* this."

This is of course the opposite view to killing many ideas and just ending up with a few.

But it is interesting to note that the majority of the great companies with a reputation for creativity and innovation (such as Virgin and Procter & Gamble) tried many things first and just kept the winners.

When it comes to creativity, so called 'Aha'
or 'Eureka' moments are extremely unusual.

According to Steven Johnson, bestselling author
of *Where Good Ideas Come From*, most great
ideas start with a hunch and slowly develop.

It all starts when you 'brief yourself'.

This is you telling your depth mind, or
sub-conscious, what the task in hand is.

Don't expect fireworks immediately.

And don't labour over it too much; the
harder you think, the worse it can get.

If you write down the rough idea, it is more likely
to emerge as a breakthrough later.

Probably when you are doing something
different entirely, which is why so many
people have excellent ideas when they are
in the shower, jogging, or painting a wall.

Have confidence in the slow hunch.

Everybody loves new stuff.

For some reason, it's usually more interesting than the old stuff.

But companies need to beware of novelty overload.

New ideas fight for attention, time and resources, and can prove very distracting if not properly channeled.

The knack is to pursue ruthless pruning of projects, and a healthy cynicism about the amount of time and resource a new idea will soak up.

"I had a monumental idea this morning, but I didn't like it."

So said Samuel Goldwyn, founder of the Metro-Goldwyn-Mayer film company.

It takes courage to recognize something for what it is, and then reject it if necessary in the interests of the greater good.

So, next time you or your team has an apparently brilliant idea, first consider rejecting it.

Sometimes, there is no point in carrying on.

In business, this thought can lend two
helpful perspectives.

First, some people and companies simply don't
want to give up what they have had up till now.

This may be the right thing to do, but where
creativity is required, hanging on to old ways is
rarely productive.

Second, when everyone has become far too
committed to something that clearly isn't working,
then pulling out can be the best option.

Although painful, quitting is better than persisting
with something sub-standard.

Pulling the plug on any project requires bravery,
particularly when everyone has invested so
much time and effort.

But sometimes it's the right thing to do.

Martina Navratilova was described as "the greatest singles, doubles, and mixed doubles player who's ever lived."

That was some compliment, coming from former World Number One player Billie Jean King.

This is what Martina had to say about commitment:

"Other players are involved in tennis, but I'm committed. It's like ham and eggs. The chicken is involved; the pig is committed."

So there you have it. If you want to push creativity to the limit, you need to be fully committed.

There's no point in going into it half-hearted.

In fact, if you do find yourself losing enthusiasm, then you might reasonably conclude that the idea is not good enough.

So try harder.

A 'Done' Wall is something proposed by Scott Belsky in his book *Making Ideas Happen*.

Done Walls are a highly motivating idea.

Put everything the team has done on the wall as massive checklists, thereby continually reminding everyone of how much progress has been made.

It makes the place look like a productivity factory, so no one sits around worrying that they are not getting anywhere.

Beware that there is a huge difference between these true steps of progress and other irrelevant stuff that has no real bearing on forward motion.

Procrastinators typically do far too much insecurity work — stuff with no intended outcome that is quick enough to do, without them (or anyone else) realizing that it's actually a waste of time.

So the Done Wall is the home of genuinely helpful pieces of progress that confirm to everyone that you are really getting somewhere.

According to the American educator John Morrison:
"Knowledge comes by taking things apart: analysis.
But wisdom comes by putting things together."

So you need to know enough about something to
understand it, and then, once you have analysed
and understood it, you can start imagining
something new.

As we have seen, creativity does not have to
be staggeringly original – just an intelligent step
to improve something or solve a problem in a
different way.

As the philosopher Daniel Dennett said:
"What you can imagine depends on what
you know."

This is somewhat in contrast to novelist
William Goldman, who nihilistically claimed:
"Nobody knows anything."

Imagining something is just the beginning.
The crucial next step is to get down to work.

Chuck Close is an American painter who makes massive-scale photorealist portraits. In his opinion: "Inspiration is for amateurs. The rest of us just show up and get to work."

In other words, it is pointless sitting around waiting for inspiration to strike, because it doesn't happen unless you get down to work.

That could be writing, painting, building – anything that begins whatever you are working on.

Comic book writer Stan Lee agrees: "I don't have inspiration. I only have ideas. Ideas and deadlines."

So inspiration is a somewhat elusive and ethereal concept. Don't assume it will come as a matter of course.

Typically, it doesn't. But circumstances can have a huge effect on the likelihood of ideas emerging. For example, being bored is excellent for creativity.

We will leave the last word on this to architect Mark Kirkhart: "I have ideas I haven't even had yet."

A WORD ON RELATIONSHIPS

Take the issues seriously, but not yourself.

Think carefully about how you come across and
how you interact with others.

Anticipate reactions to your actions.

Be open-minded and receptive to a broad range
of opinions, and respect those you work with
and their differing views.

Remember that small things can make a big difference,
and pay attention to how you use your time and
other people's time. Don't be a time thief.

You can't do everything yourself, so respect the
decisions of others when you were not involved.

Don't compare yourself to others – just be a first-rate
version of yourself.

As Jim Rohn said, "You are the average of the
five people you spend most time with."

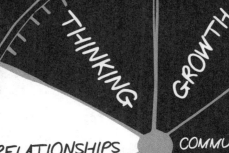

PART FIVE

"All jokes will be taken seriously."
Border crossing sign.

There are some really serious people around.

To them, everything is such a big deal.

Hubris. Self-aggrandizement. Arrogance. Pomposity.
Self-importance.

Call it what you like. But it doesn't have to
be this way.

It's perfectly possible to approach issues seriously
whilst still adopting a light touch to personalities
and people.

A little self-deprecation goes a long way.

We don't all have to be gun slinging, brash,
world-beating executives.

In fact, none of us should be really.

So when it comes to work, take the issues seriously,
but not yourself.

This simple question works in two very different directions.

Both are highly poignant.

First, directed inward to yourself: "What's in it for me?"

This is a critical way to work out whether you want to do something or not.

If you see no satisfaction in the task or project, then try to avoid it.

Second, put yourself in the shoes of the other person, and imagine them asking: "What's in it for me?"

If you cannot generate a satisfactory answer on their behalf, then the other person is unlikely to agree with you, or be satisfied with what you are asking them to do.

People have to be sufficiently motivated in order to agree with you or perform well.

It might be a financial point, but more often it is simply a matter of motivation.

The French philosopher Simone Weil said: "Humility is attentive patience."

Humility goes a long way.

And yet many managers are strident, hectoring, macho, and domineering.

It's not good enough.

It's completely unnecessary. And it's not even an effective technique.

You might think that there are benefits to this approach, but there are none.

So, companies should be in search of managers with modesty. People who don't have to show off regularly.

Or brag incessantly.

Or always take the credit.

So if you are hiring, look for modesty.

And if you are managing people, show some humility and spread the joy a bit.

Working out likely cause and effect only takes a few seconds.

Consider for a moment: "If I do x, then y will (almost certainly) happen."

You can then analyze whether y is desirable or not, before you act.

If y is desirable, then do x.

If y is irrelevant or inconsequential, then still do x.

If y is not desirable, then don't do x.

This last one is arguably the hardest.

Too many people do things that will clearly have undesired consequences, but they still do them anyway.

Pausing to think for just a few seconds can remove thousands of instances of this happening.

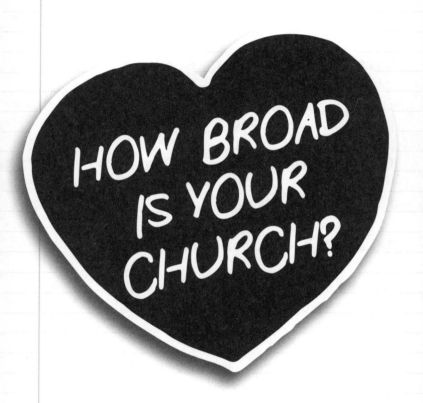

A broad church has lots of different types of people in it.

Variety is not only welcomed, but actively encouraged.

So when you are putting teams together, do not hire in your own image.

You will simply end up with lots of mini versions of you.

Doubtless they will have all your talents and traits, but also all your faults and deficiencies.

"Hire character. Train skill."

So said Peter Schutz, the Chief Executive of Porsche.

Be open-minded about different styles, and embrace them to create a richly diverse team.

Then allocate the right tasks to the right people.

You can't ask nine women to make a baby in a month.

Dividing up work arbitrarily doesn't necessarily mean faster and better results.

You need the right people doing the right stuff.

Polar explorer Roald Amundsen beat Captain Scott to the South Pole by consistently marching 20 miles a day.

He had worked out in advance that 20 miles was the optimum amount for a team with their equipment.

In bad weather the team did it anyway, and in good they stopped at 20 to save energy for the next day.

Scott's team either stayed in their tents on bad days or overshot on good ones and wore themselves out.

The moral is that companies, teams and individuals should aim for similar consistency.

This is what the business authors Collins and Hansen call "fanatic discipline".

Don't ease off just because things are difficult, or overdo it when things are easy.

Apply consistent 20 mile marches, and ask the same of your colleagues.

SMALL THINGS = BIG DIFFERENCE

It seems the world is obsessed with everything being BIG. Old joke:

Texan: "Where I come from boy, I can drive all day and still be on my own land."

Englishman: "Yeah, I had a car like that once."

Big doesn't necessarily mean good. It could even be bad.

By contrast, there are tremendous advantages to making small changes.

Behavioural science has shown that tiny variations in phraseology can cause huge change.

Small changes are usually less costly, and often free.

Small changes attract less attention from bosses and meddlers, so they are easier to implement.

Small changes are easier to rectify if they don't achieve their original objective.

So bear in mind that the 'next big thing' could be small.

Being personable costs nothing and makes your working life more pleasant.

It also makes it better for everyone else.

Constructive, thoughtful people attract more of the same.

They give and earn respect.

Which means a calmer, less stressed working environment.

Part of the knack is always having time to help out a colleague.

So when they ask if you have a minute to discuss something, the answer should, within reason, be yes.

This level of respect and attentiveness also allows you to be candid without being brusque.

As actress and comedian Amy Poehler says:

"If you can speak about what you care about to a person you disagree with without denigrating them, then you may actually be heard."

That's good news for everybody.

Ever been to an important meeting where someone (often the most senior person) failed to turn up?

The meeting proceeds, and the people who did have the courtesy to turn up agree something productive and useful.

Some time later, the senior person who wasn't there overrules or ignores the recommendation that the team has made.

This is not on.

No show = no say.

In other words, if you can't be bothered to turn up, then you forfeit your right to contribute, let alone exert a power of veto.

Senior managers need to heed this.

Breathlessly lurching from meeting to meeting poorly briefed and under prepared, or failing to make it at all, is dysfunctional behaviour.

Even worse, if you never made the meeting at all, then at least respect your people by letting them get on with it.

There's a Meat Loaf song called 'Everything Louder Than Everything Else'.

This is roughly how many people operate in business, especially frenetic bosses.

They want full throttle on everything.

They initiate too many projects.

They want their staff working all hours on all fronts.

They don't set a single objective. They set multiple ones.

And they want it all now, or possibly even yesterday.

This leaves everyone confused, and incapable of knowing what to deal with next.

Setting clear priorities is critical.

Be ruthless on tasks, remove low priority items, and set people running on one thing at a time.

BE A FIRST-RATE VERSION OF YOURSELF

It was Judy Garland who said this: "Always be a first-rate version of yourself and not a second-rate version of someone else."

Far too many people spend too much time comparing themselves with everyone else, but that isn't really the important thing.

You need to be yourself.

Then your style and talents can come to the fore and really contribute to the team.

Few people work in total isolation, and outcomes are always stronger and better when they are looked at by a diverse range of people.

To be your best self, you need to know what you stand for. As the late actor Chadwick Boseman pointed out: "Sometimes you need to get knocked down before you can really figure out what your fight is."

You can be certain of yourself when you know what your struggle is.

Even if you don't, actress Lillian Hellman reckons that: "It is best to act with confidence, no matter how little right you have to it."

You can be kind and considerate in your relationships, and that's fine.

But you also need strength of purpose and sufficient conviction to stick to your guns when you encounter resistance to your approach or ideas.

The Russian-American writer and philosopher Ayn Rand was tough on this: "The question isn't who is going to let me; it's who is going to stop me."

However, this kind of approach to prevailing over the opinions of others comes with a health warning: tenaciously clinging on to a belief despite contrary evidence can be a mistake.

Scientists and physicians are frequently guilty of this, putting up what Paul Feltovich calls "knowledge shields" to allow them to stick to their original diagnoses even when subsequently proven wrong.

Conviction is good, and overcoming resistance takes tenacity – so long as you have enough humility to admit when you are wrong.

A WORD ON THINKING

Thinking is free, so do it more often.

Make sure you allocate plenty of regular time to think.
That comes first. Only then will you know what to do.

Don't forget that, sometimes, doing nothing is
the best option.

Tame your technology, and develop the vital habit
of saying no, politely, to too many requests.

Efficiency is a sophisticated form of laziness,
so practise discipline in the way you work.

Think, but don't overthink.

And do not make yourself busy for the sake of
being busy. Effective business does not equate
to busyness.

Author Alice Munro believes, "The constant
happiness is curiosity."

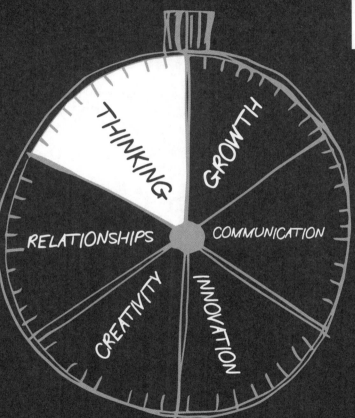

PART SIX

THINKING

GROWTH

RELATIONSHIPS

COMMUNICATION

CREATIVITY

INNOVATION

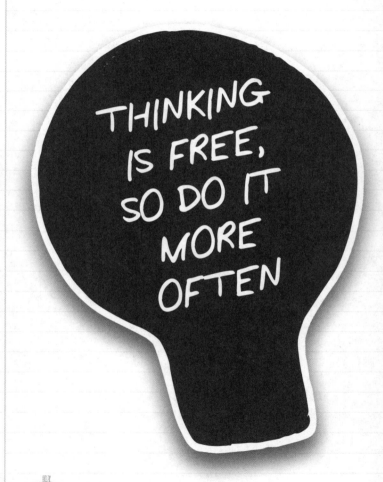

Many people claim that they have no time to think.

It's a poor excuse.

Thinking needn't take very long.

It's totally free, and it's probably the most powerful asset that you have.

Novelist Victor Hugo once said:

"You can resist an army, but not an idea whose time has come."

A good idea can move a lot of people.

More humbly, thinking clearly will prevent you from doing lots of things that you don't believe in, or that won't get you very far.

On certain days when you do not have wall-to-wall meetings, this is a small mantra that works really well.

Sit and think.

When you have thought of something,
do it immediately.

Keep doing this all day, until you have cleared
all the small details from your mind, or your
task list.

You can apply the same principle to reviewing your business, looking at many areas and making a list.

Divide the tasks into subject areas, or those to
do with one particular colleague, and tackle them
each in turn.

This approach is better than multi-tasking,
which has been proven not to work well.

Rapid Sequential Tasking works better.

Do something, finish it, then move on fast
to the next thing.

Maverick Brazilian businessman Ricardo Semler suggests that when anything untoward happens you should do nothing on the assumption that good sense will eventually sort it out.

It's good advice.

Far too many situations are enflamed by tit-for-tat reactions.

If you follow the principle of "If I do x, then y will happen," then you should be able to predict that sequence quite easily.

From a different perspective, too much business activity isn't productive.

There are plenty of instances when whole companies, let alone teams and individuals, would have been better off doing nothing at all.

If that sounds absurd, how do we explain a company with 10,000 employees who work hard all year only to make a loss?

So, next time you are contemplating some frenetic activity, consider doing nothing.

The best way to analyze a task is to work out whether it is quantitative or qualitative.

Quantitative tasks can neither be done well nor badly. They are just stuff. And usually there is a greater quantity of them.

Qualitative tasks require more thought. They usually take longer and they can certainly be done very well or very badly.

Sit down with your checklist and divide all your tasks into these two types.

Then allocate suitable bursts of time to tackle them.

Your choice of time slot is often a blend of your personal style and the rhythm of your business.

For example, some people like to have a quant blast first thing on a Monday, or on a sweep-up Friday.

Qual tasks need to be planned carefully in the diary, and not violated at the last minute by trivia.

TAME YOUR TECHNOLOGY

Technology has changed the way we work and live, and it controls us more than we are prepared to admit.

"The Ping" is author Todd Henry's expression for being distracted — the little feeling that makes you check your email for no particular reason.

We need to learn to pay attention to what is in front of us rather than what might be happening elsewhere.

Most of us these days suffer from Continuous Partial Attention.

We are always fiddling around and convincing ourselves that we can 'multi-task' effectively.

We can't.

We need to set about taming our technology.

That means understanding the true effect it has on our behaviour, and making changes to counteract it.

Switch your machines off from time to time, and if you want to get something important done, leave your computer and do it in peace.

There are many ways to say no without using the word no.

Most involve asking a new question, or reframing the request.

The most powerful way is to offer an alternative that is better.

The benefit of this is that many tasks that you are asked to do can be turned into something more interesting or avoided altogether.

And you will have been polite and constructive all along.

Of course, there are times when you will be told no.

When that happens, treat it as a request for further information.

As Bob Gill of Pringles said:

"They don't really mean 'No' – they just haven't understood it as well as you have."

So it's your job to keep informing them until they say yes.

Being effective in business doesn't always have to mean being perpetually busy.

Business does not have to equal busyness.

In fact, it absolutely shouldn't.

If you are running around all day then you'll have no time to think.

Instead, as the business writer Michael E. Gerber suggests, you should:

"Go to work ON the business, rather than IN it."

That means dedicating enough quality time to thinking about the important issues.

Until those are grappled with, the rest is just administrivia.

EFFICIENCY
IS A
SOPHISTICATED
FORM OF
LAZINESS

The more organized you are, the more you can relax. That might not mean being lazy, but it might not be far off.

Here's the logic.

If you take the time to organize a day, a week, a project, or any other task, you can then proceed in an orderly fashion and get on with it.

In the right order, all in good time.

That reduces the need to flap around at the last minute. Which gives you more thinking time, or lazing around time if that's what you prefer.

As poet Ron Serino said: "Freely chosen, discipline is absolute freedom."

It's a virtuous circle.

It is, however, important to note that it does not work the other way round.

Lazing around for ages and then expecting everything to fall into place at the last minute doesn't work.

The relaxation or calmness only follows when the organizational work has been done.

A lot of people sit around worrying that they are not achieving their goals.

This could be an individual, a product or brand, or an entire company.

Worrying is unproductive.

It uses up huge amounts of time and creates stress.

So you might as well use the time instead to pretend that you already have what you want.

Although this sounds fanciful, and possibly even a waste of time, in fact it enables you to envisage the successful outcome that you crave.

Sports psychologists have shown that successful sports people have already pictured themselves winning.

So, to increase the clarity of your ambition, pretend that you already have what you want.

It might be fantasy, but then so might the thing you are currently worrying about.

LOOK EVERYTHING UP, WRITE EVERYTHING DOWN

Being constantly curious is a prerequisite of any successful and creative businessperson.

If you don't understand something, don't just gloss over it. Find out.

If you don't know how something works, find out.

If you don't know the meaning of a word, look it up.

If you can't remember everything, write it down.

Keep a notebook.

Be a mental magpie. Be on the lookout for interesting stimuli.

Practice serendipity.

The more you think, the more it appears that you are (apparently) 'in the right place at the right time'.

Inquisitiveness coupled with diligent recordkeeping is a powerful combination.

Look everything up, and write everything down.

Here's a joke from American comedian Demetri Martin: "The other day I was thinking, 'I just overthink things.' And then I thought, 'Do I, though?'"

That's mental circularity for you.

There are times when thinking too much is detrimental.

Obsessing over something can be unhealthy, and even counterproductive.

If you overthink something rather than just think clearly about it, you can actually *unthink* it and end up back where you started.

Blaise Pascal, the French mathematician, said: "All of man's misery comes from his incapacity to sit alone in an empty quiet room."

Thoughts usually lead to actions. And actions have consequences.

Think, but don't overthink.

Red Cross founder Clara Barton said:
"I cannot afford the luxury of a closed mind."

People with closed minds rarely make any progress. They have set their views, and they have stopped learning.

The writer Harold Acton amusingly noted that:
"Some people take no mental exercise other than jumping to conclusions."

Mental exercise is essential for the development of the mind, and for all the provocations in this book. And that means getting out of your comfort zone.

"I don't like to be out of my comfort zone, which is about a half an inch wide,"
said comedian Larry David.

You need a point of view, not just a collection of facts. As advertising expert Dave Trott points out:
"This is the problem with data: people avoid the discomfort of thinking."

Take mental exercise and always stay open-minded.

BIBLIOGRAPHY

Creative Blindness, Dave Trott (Harriman House, 2019)

Eating The Big Fish, Adam Morgan (John Wiley, 1999)

Execution, Bossidy & Charan (Crown Business, 2002)

Factfulness, Hans Rosling (Sceptre, 2019)

Great By Choice, Collins & Hansen (Random House, 2011)

Imagine, Jonah Lehrer (Canongate, 2012)

Making Ideas Happen, Scott Belsky (Portfolio Penguin, 2011)

On Bullshit, Harry G. Frankfurt (Harvard Business Review Press, 2005)

Playing To Win, Lafley & Martin (Harvard Business Review Press, 2013)

The Accidental Creative, Todd Henry (Portfolio Penguin, 2011)

The E Myth Revisited, Michael E. Gerber (Harper Collins, 1995)

The First Mile, Scott D. Anthony (Harvard Business Review Press, 2014)

The Innovation Book, Max McKeown (Pearson, 2014)

The Pirate Inside, Adam Morgan (John Wiley, 2004)

To Sell Is Human, Daniel Pink (Canongate, 2012)

Where Good Ideas Come From, Steven Johnson (Penguin, 2010)

ABOUT THE AUTHOR

KEVIN DUNCAN is a business adviser, marketing expert, motivational speaker and author. After 20 years in advertising and direct marketing, he has spent the last 20 years as an independent troubleshooter, advising companies on how to change their businesses for the better.

Contact the author for advice, training, or speaking opportunities:
kevinduncanexpertadvice@gmail.com
expertadviceonline.com | thesmartthinkingbook.com

ALSO BY THE AUTHOR:

Business Greatest Hits

How To Run And Grow Your Own Business

How To Tame Technology And Get Your Life Back

Marketing Greatest Hits

Marketing Greatest Hits Volume 2

Revolution

Run Your Own Business

Small Business Survival

So What?

Start

Start Your Own Business

The Business Bullshit Book

The Diagrams Book

The Dictionary of Business Bullshit

The Excellence Book

The Ideas Book

The Intelligent Work Book

The Smart Strategy Book

Tick Achieve

What You Need To Know About Starting A Business

FOR OTHER TITLES IN THE SERIES...

CONCISE
ADVICE
LAB

SMALL BOOKS: BIG IDEAS

CLEVER CONTENT, DYNAMIC IDEAS, PRACTICAL
SOLUTIONS AND ENGAGING VISUALS –
A CATALYST TO INSPIRE NEW WAYS OF THINKING
AND PROBLEM-SOLVING IN A COMPLEX WORLD

conciseadvicelab.com